Amazing Adults Colouring Book
GUERNSEY

Illustrated by
Jacq le Breton
Printed by
CreateSpace

Little Chapel

Puffins

Les Hanois

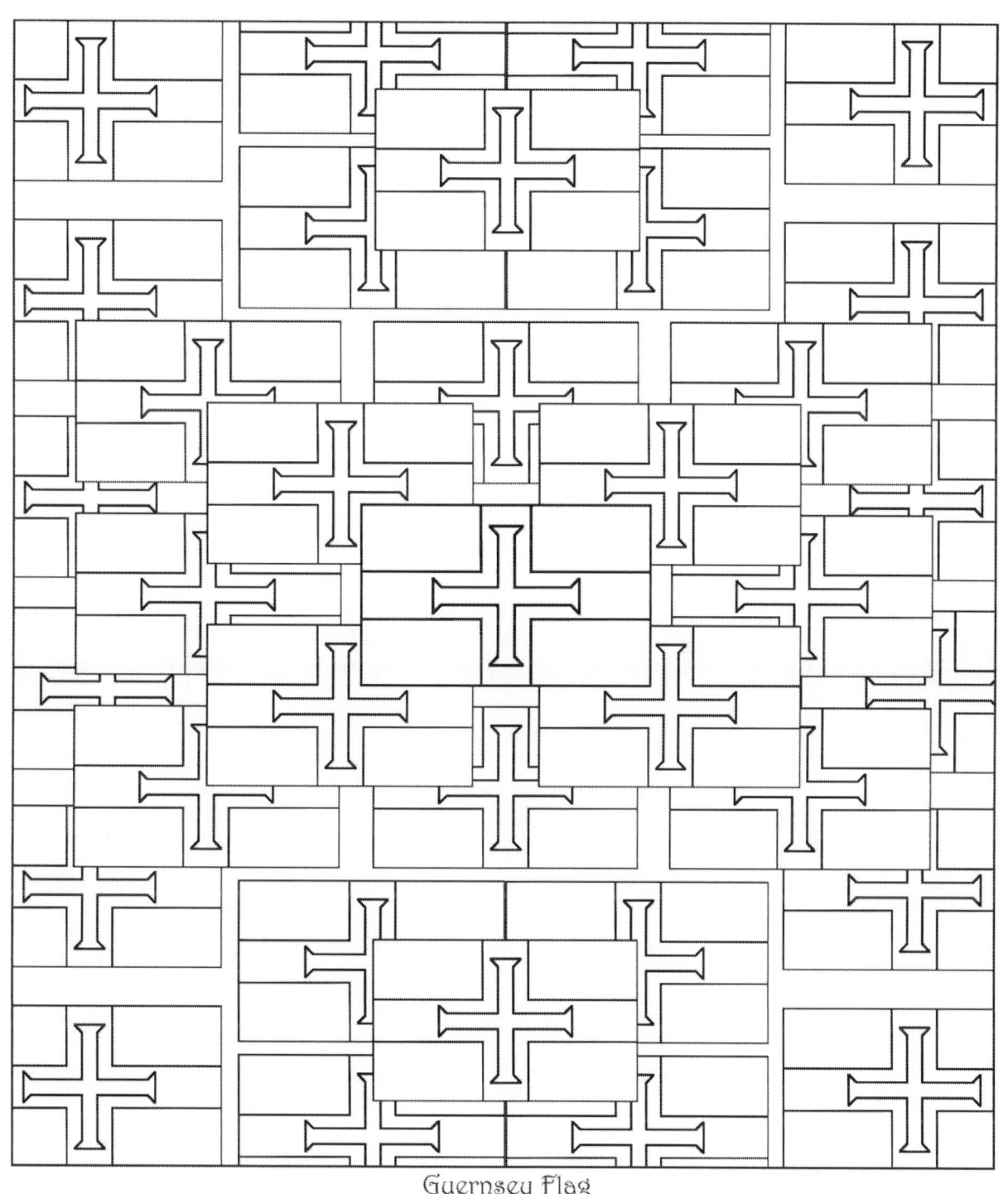

Guernsey Flag

Bean Jar

Martello tower

Guernsey crest

Victoria Tower

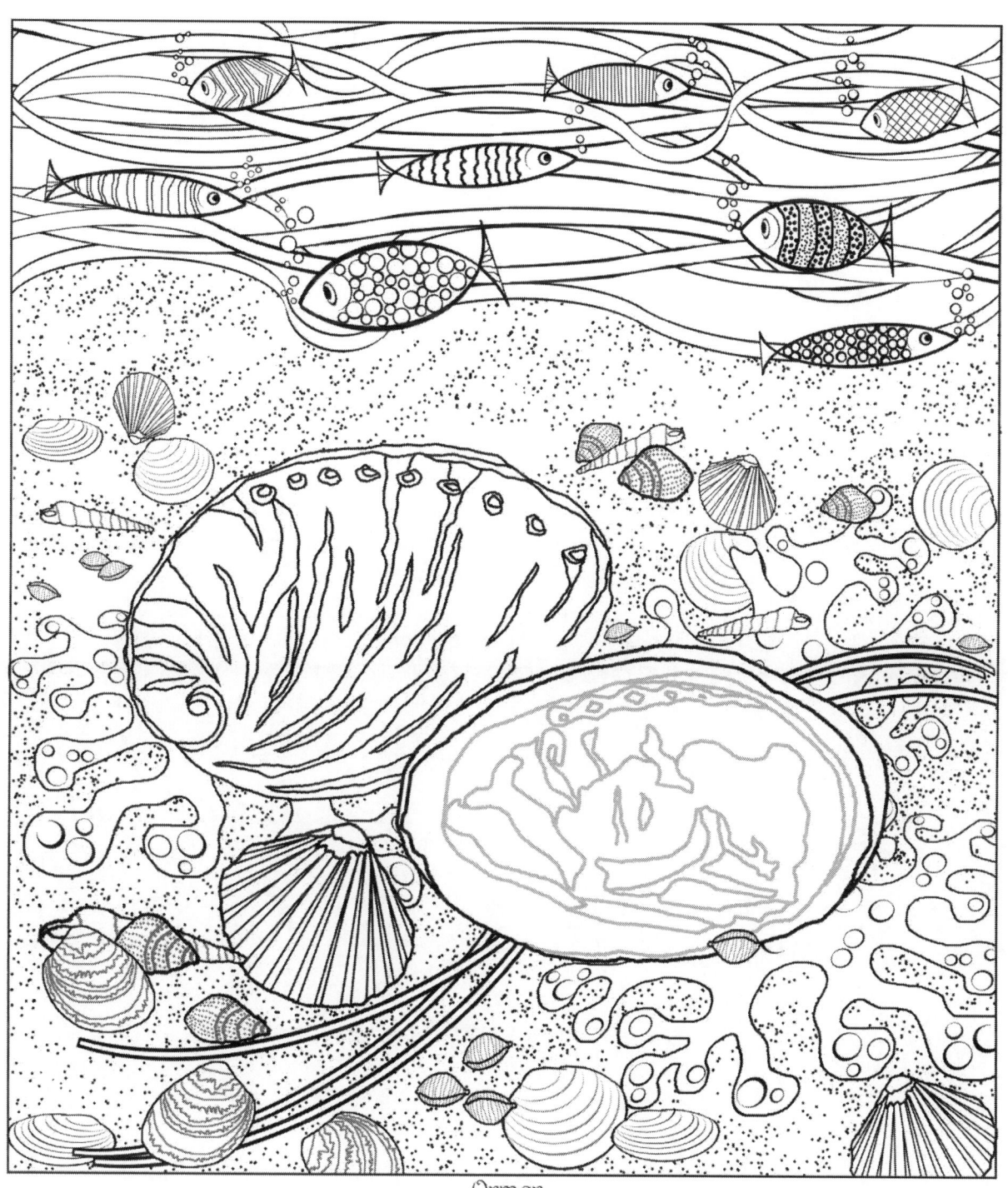

Ormer

Nerine Sarniensis

Guernsey milk can

Sunken Gardens War Memorial

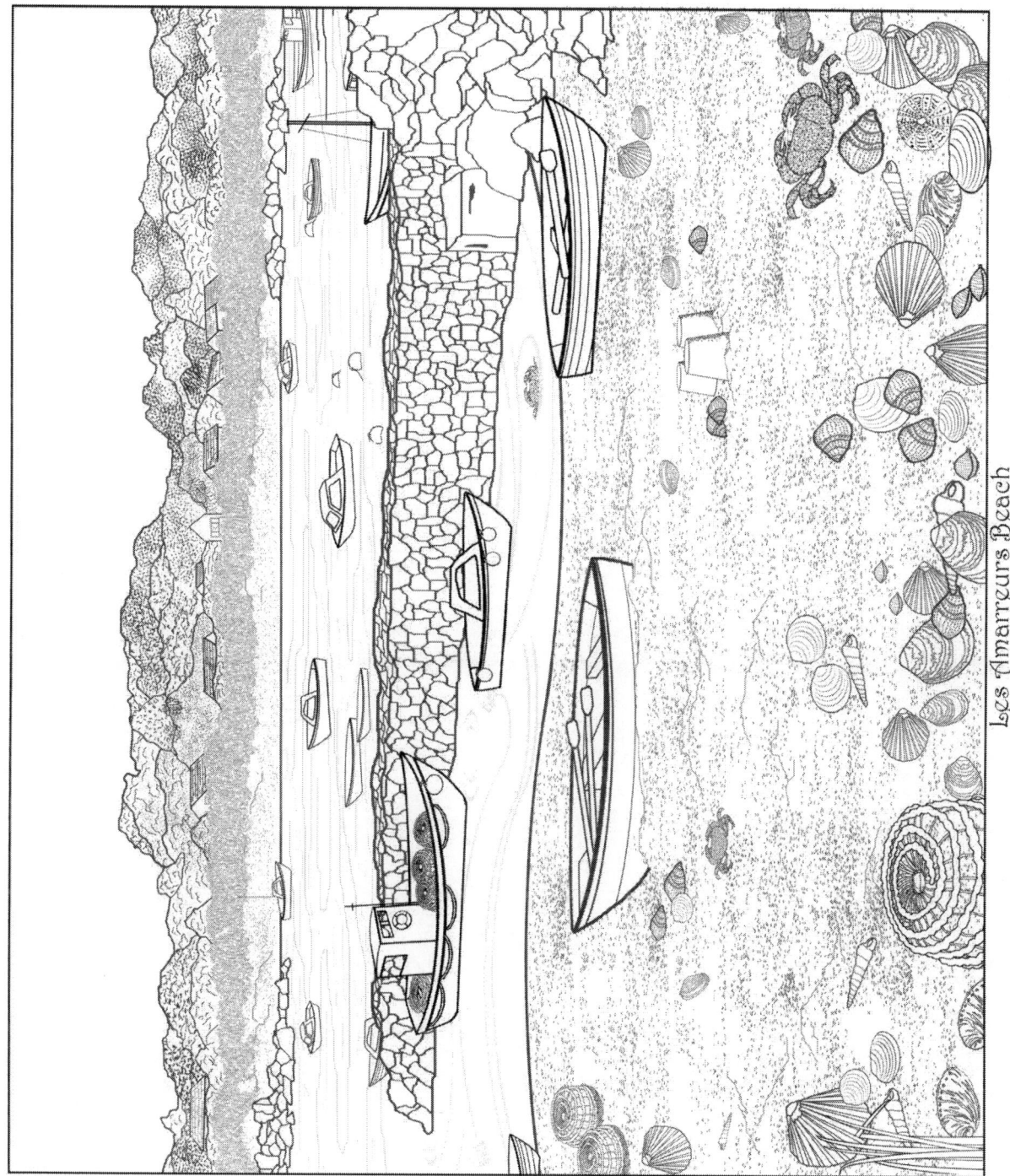

Les Amarreurs Beach

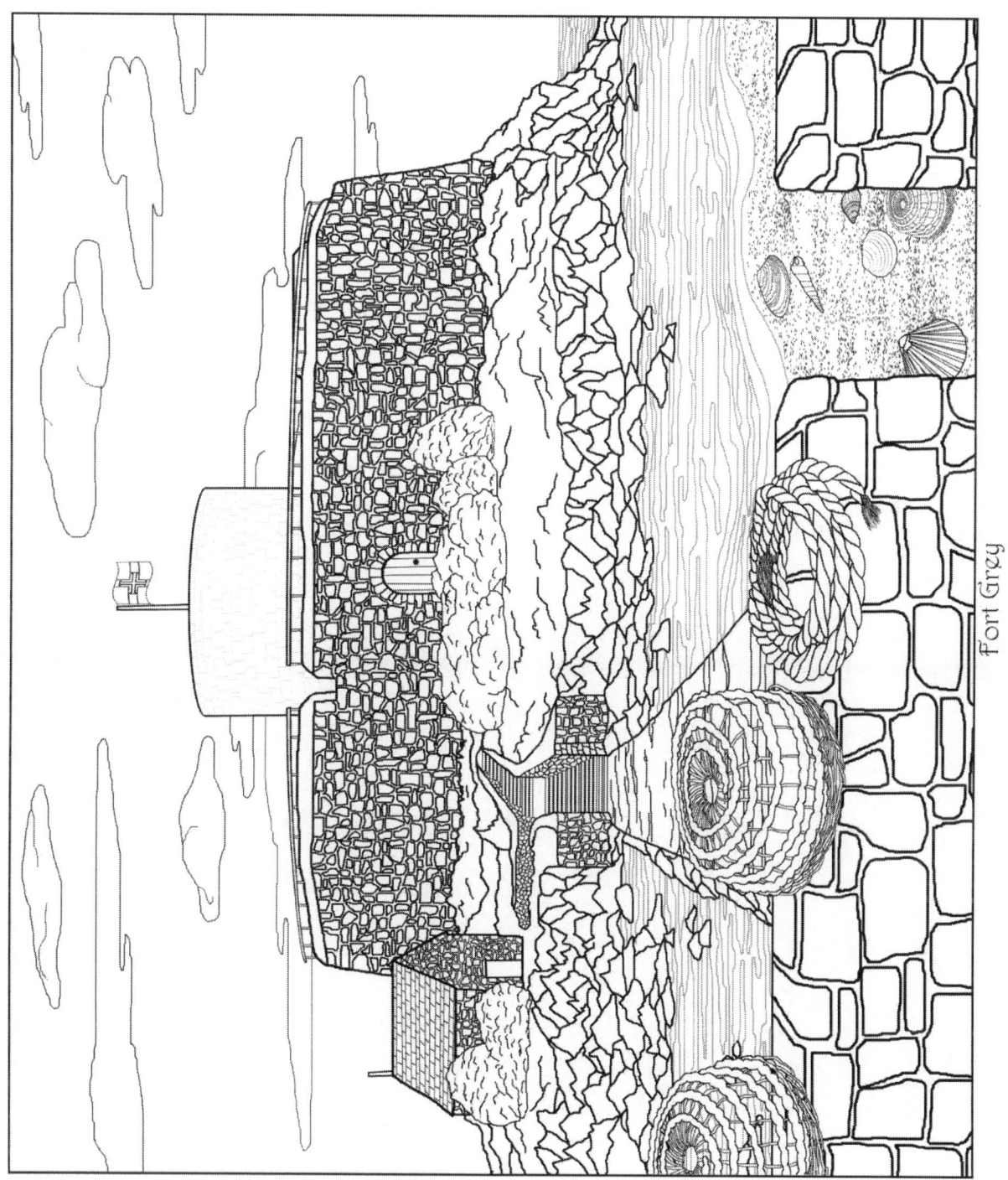

Fort Grey

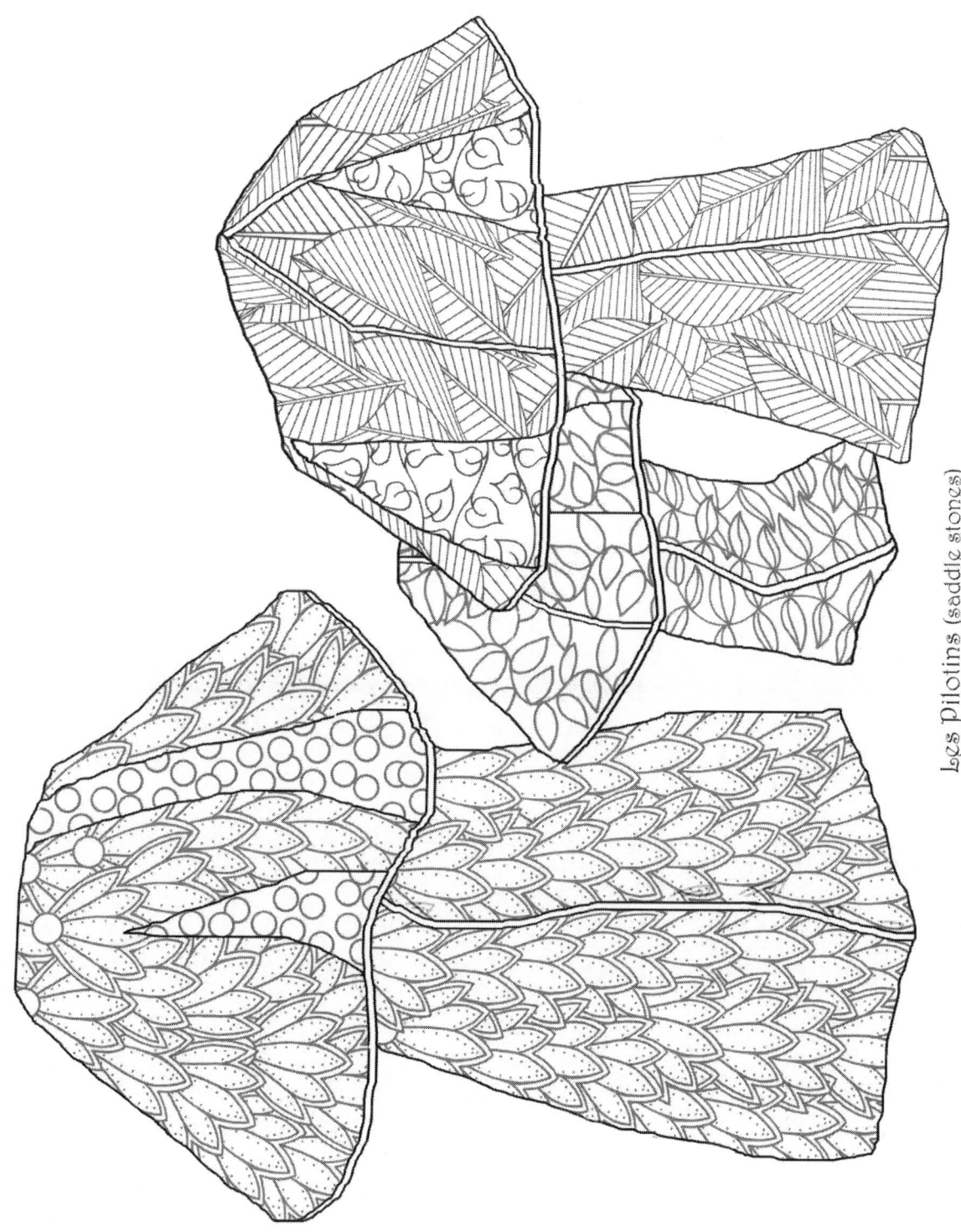

Les Pilotins (saddle stones)

Town Church

Golden Guernsey goat

La Table des Pions

Guernsey cottage

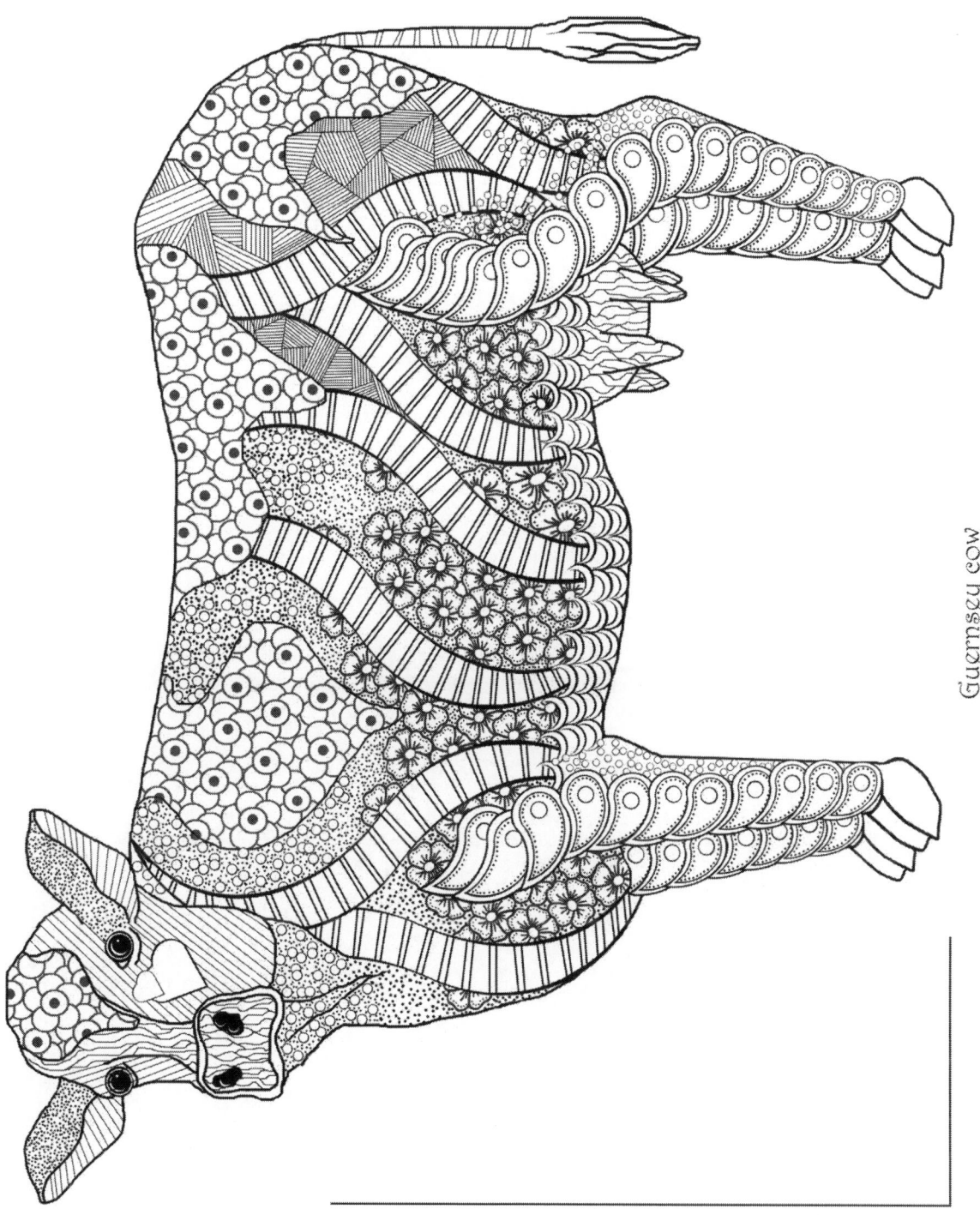

Guernsey cow

Sunken Gardens War Memorial

Castle Cornet

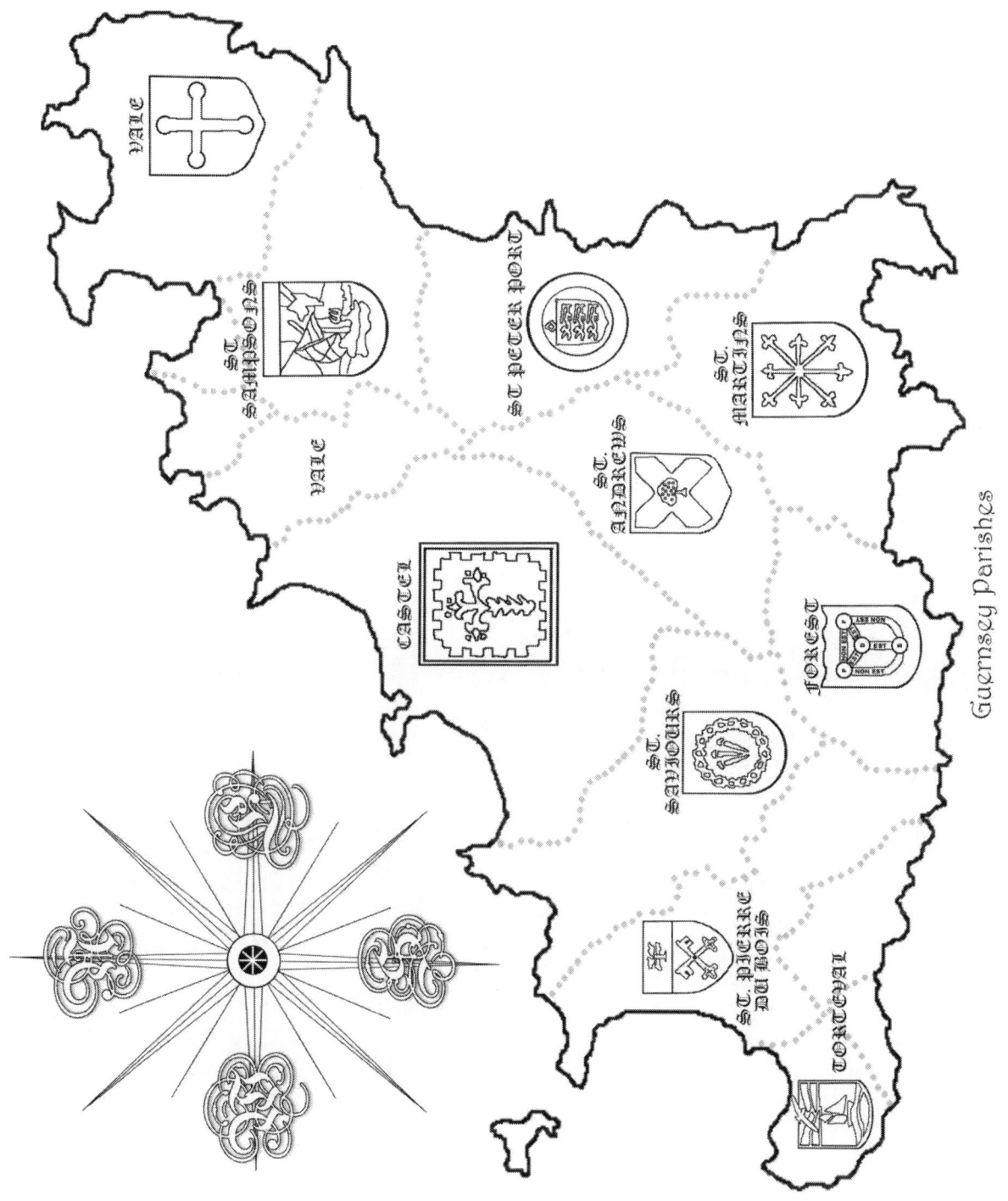

Guernsey Parishes

17746938R00028

Printed in Great Britain
by Amazon